Brain

Lisa Greathouse

Consultant

Gina Montefusco, RN
Children's Hospital Los Angeles
Los Angeles, California

Publishing Credits

Dona Herweck Rice, *Editor-in-Chief*; Lee Aucoin, *Creative Director*; Don Tran, *Print Production Manager*; Timothy J. Bradley, *Illustration Manager*; Chris McIntyre, *Editorial Director*; James Anderson, *Associate Editor*; Jamey Acosta, *Associate Editor*; Neri Garcia, *Sebior Designer*; Peter Balaskas, *Editorial Administrator*; Stephanie Reid, *Photo Editor*; Jane Gould, *Editor*; Rachelle Cracchiolo, *M.S.Ed., Publisher*

Teacher Created Materials

5301 Oceanus Drive
Huntington Beach, CA 92649-1030
http://www.tcmpub.com
ISBN 978-1-4333-1428-5

Table of Contents

Your Amazing Brain

Do you remember the last book you read? Do you know why you should not touch a hot stove? Can you think of your best friend's last name?

Have you ever wondered how you know all of the things you know? You can thank your brain!

Your Brain, the Boss

Your brain controls everything you think, say, and do. It keeps your heart beating, and it makes sure you are breathing.

Your brain looks like a slimy, gray sponge. It only weighs about three pounds, but it is the boss of your whole body!

Just Like Us

Your brain is about the size of a dolphin's brain!

Have you ever stubbed your toe and wondered why it hurts so much? There are nerves all over your body. They are connected to your brain.

When you stub your toe, the nerves in your toe send a message to your brain. That message says, "Ouch!"

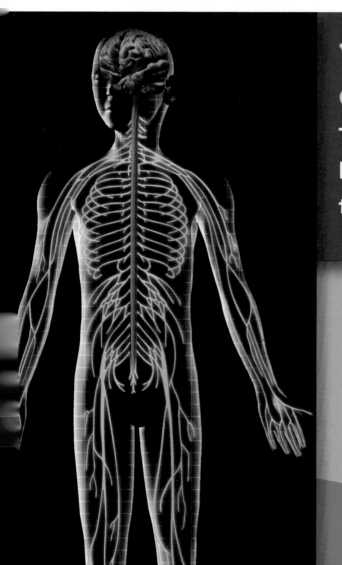

You Have a LOT of Nerve!

The nerves in your body look like long, thin branches.

So how does that pain in your toe get all the way to your brain so fast? The brain gets help from the **spinal cord**.

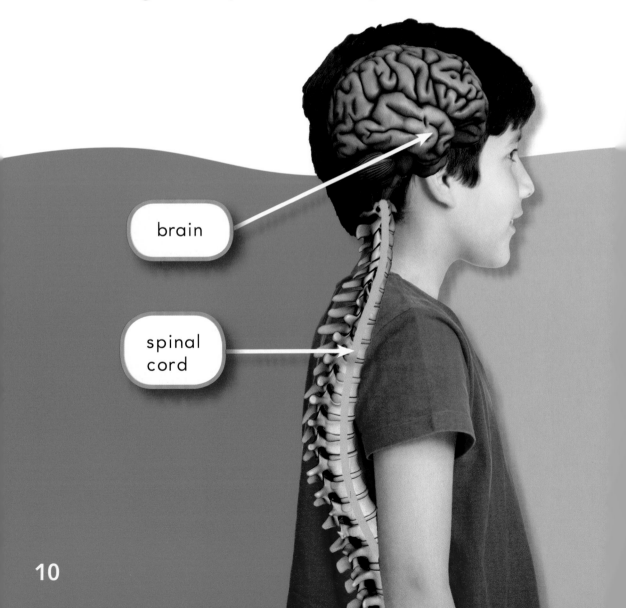

brain

spinal cord

The spinal cord runs down your back.
It meets the brain at the top of your
neck. It delivers messages to your brain.

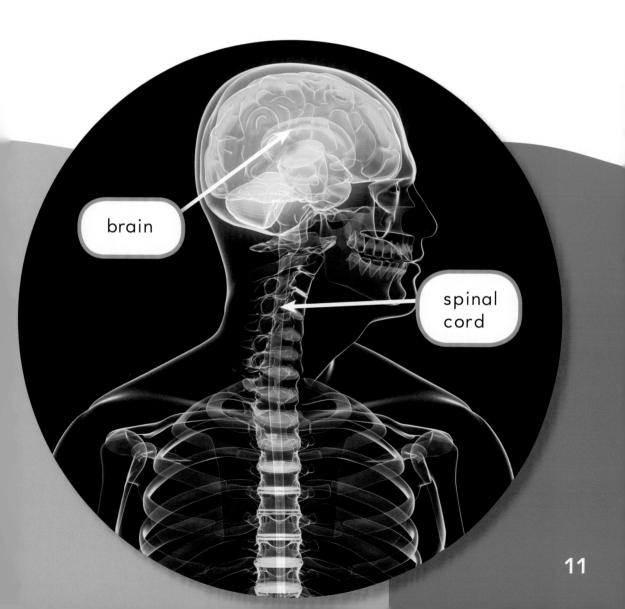

brain

spinal
cord

One Brain, Many Parts

Your brain has many parts and each part has a job. The biggest part of the brain is called the **cerebrum** (suh-REE-brum). It is in charge of thinking.

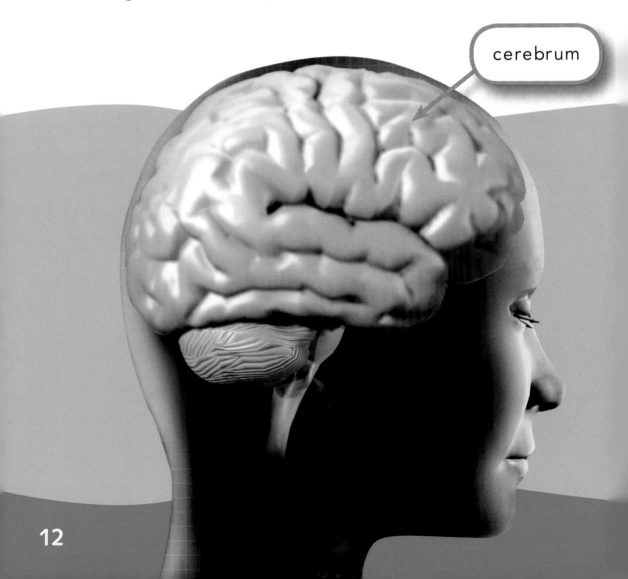

cerebrum

The cerebrum also helps you move your body. You cannot hit a baseball or solve a math problem without it!

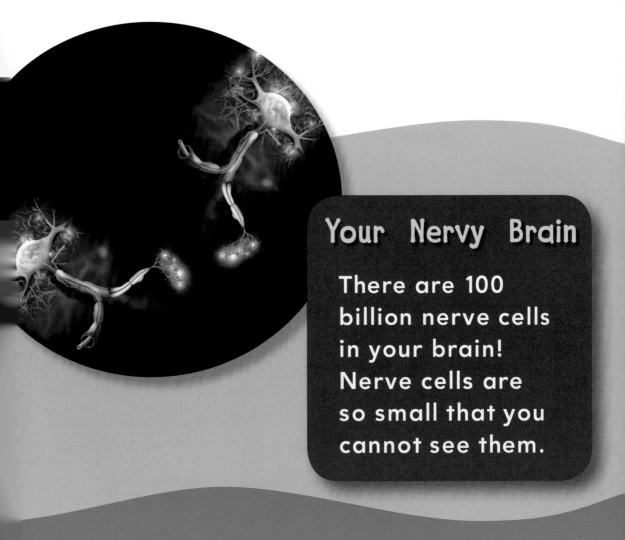

Your Nervy Brain

There are 100 billion nerve cells in your brain! Nerve cells are so small that you cannot see them.

You never have to think about breathing. That is the job of another part of your brain called the **brain stem**.

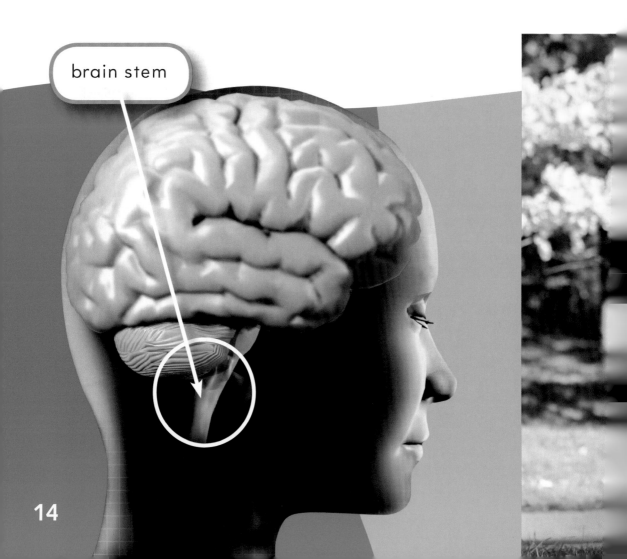

brain stem

The brain stem has a big job. It tells your heart to pump more blood when you are running. It even tells your stomach to digest your lunch!

It Is All in Your Head!

What kind of **mood** are you in today? Ask your brain!

It is your brain that makes you sad when you cannot go out and play. It makes you happy on your birthday. And it is not your heart that tells you that you love your family. It is your brain!

Look at the faces of people. Can you tell their moods?

You may think that you can see because of your eyes, but your brain plays a big part, too.

First, your eyes see something. Then, the nerves in your eyes send a message to the brain. It is the brain that figures out what you are seeing.

Brain Flip

Eyes see things upside down. It is a good thing the brain knows to flip the image!

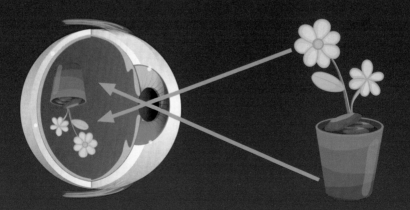

Each time you learn something, your brain gets stronger. Remember the first time you rode a bike? You were not very good at first, were you?

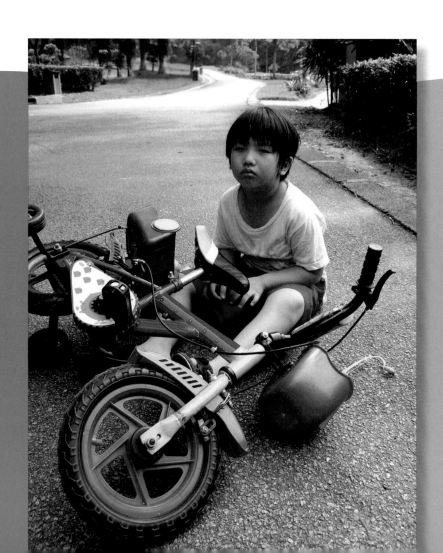

You had to practice. When you practice, you build up your brain. That is why the more you do something, the better you get.

Busy Brain!

Your brain keeps working—even when you go to sleep. That is why you have dreams.

Your brain cannot do all this work on its own. Read this list to learn some things you can do to keep your brain in great shape.

- **Eat healthy foods.**
- **Get lots of exercise.**
- **Get plenty of sleep.**
- **Read.**
- **Play music.**
- **Stay away from drugs and alcohol.**

You need to take care of your brain from the outside, too! Always wear a helmet when you ride a bike, skateboard, or scooter.

You should wear a helmet when you play some sports, too. Helmets look cool, and they help keep your brain safe!

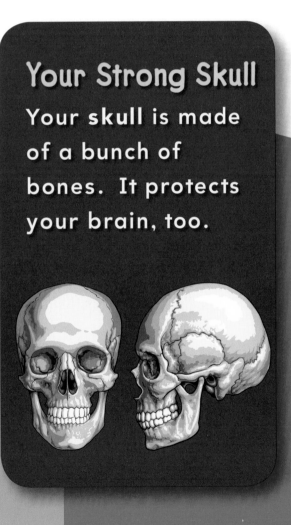

Your Strong Skull

Your **skull** is made of a bunch of bones. It protects your brain, too.

Brain Power

Now you know why your brain is the boss of your body! It stores all your memories, it tells you what to say and do, and it keeps you alive. Take care of your brain and it will take care of you!

Science Lab: Brain Box

What is in the box? If you cannot see it, how can you know?

Materials:

- a box with a hole cut in the side for your hand
- six objects with different textures, such as a spoon, a sock, a cotton ball, a block, a paperclip, and an apple
- a latex glove

Procedure:

❶ Ask someone to find objects and place them in the box. Do not peek!

❷ Put on the glove and put your hand through the hole. Feel the objects to try to guess what is in the box.

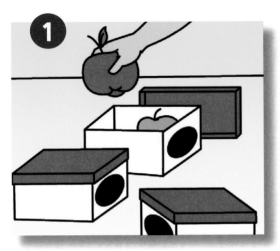

❸ Now, try again without the glove.

❹ Open the box to see what is inside.

❺ Think: Why was it harder to figure out what was in the box without your full sense of touch? What other senses would have made it easier to figure out what was in the box?

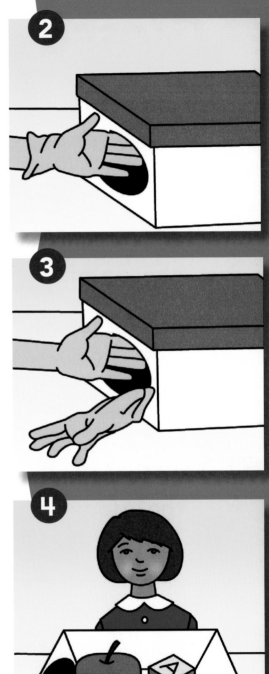

Glossary

brain stem—the part of the brain that connects the rest of the brain to the spinal cord

cerebrum—the part of the brain in charge of thinking

mood—the way a person feels

skull—the bones in the head that surround and protect the brain

spinal cord—a thick bundle of nerves that goes up the back and connects the brain to the rest of the body

Index

A Scientist Today

Dr. Jordan Tang studies the brain. He is trying to find out why some people lose their memory through disease. He is looking for ways to help them, and he is looking for a cure.